D1797289

Burnley As It Was

Ross. C. Burton

Published by: Hendon Publishing Company. © Ross C. Burton, 1972.
Printed by: Turner & Earnshaw Ltd., Bread Street, Burnley.

90p

FOREWORD

To capture the full history of Burnley's past in one book of photographs is impossible. The vast collection of photographs preserved in the Central Library alone makes any selection a very difficult choice. However, it is better to make an effort at presentation than do nothing to preserve some memories of 'BURNLEY AS IT WAS'. The young people of today are looking forward, and rightly so, but as we are all well aware, no-one stays young for ever, and sooner or later there begins a casual look back over the shoulder. For the older people, nostalgic memories often bring a warm glow, and this book is intended to give pleasure to generations of Burnleyites — young or old.

St. Peter's Church. This Church is the oldest in Burnley and dates back to the reign of King Henry the First. No part, however, of the present edifice can be said to be older than the time of Edward III. The north and middle aisles were rebuilt about A.D. 1532-33, the south aisle in 1789-90, and the tower was raised thirty feet in 1802-3. In 1872-3 the chancel was enlarged as a memorial to Sir James Yorke Scarlett, who on the 25th October, 1854, led the charge of the Heavy Brigade at the Battle of Balaclava and who died at his residence within sight of the church. Previous to the Reformation there were four altars in this Church: 1. The Rood Altar; 2. The High Altar, dedicated to St. Peter; 3. St. Mary's Altar in the Towneley Choir; and St. Anthony's Altar in the Stansfield Choir. The Towneley Chantry was founded A.D. 1373, and many illustrious members of the Towneley family are herein their "narrow cells for ever laid." The registers of the Church commence Easter. A.D. 1562. The first incumbent of whom there is any record is "Henricus", who was officiating here in the year 1200.

The original centre of Burnley in 1800, showing the Old Market Square, the Old Sparrow Hawk and Godley Lane on the left of the photograph.

The Old Shorey Well. Shorey Well close to Bank Hall was the original waterworks of Burnley. That is to say that in the days when Burnley was a little village lying around St. Peter's Church, Shorey Well filled the place of parish pump and supplied the hamlet with water. It was there people went carrying pails and other vessels to fetch the cold sparkling water for which it was famous, and one conjures up in imagination the rural simplicity of those times when Burnley people wended their way, pail and pitcher laden, to gossip with their neighbours at the parish well. Old Shorey must have occupied a very important place in Burnley life then. In later days, after a regular system of water-works were established, Old Shorey still remained in much request, for it was long before the new system of waterworks was universally adopted. Gradually, however, it fell into disuse and disrepair. It was fenced off at last because the footpath approaching it became dangerous. Then a boy playing on the riverside near it fell into the stream and was drowned, and after that the well was walled up and the path to it partly removed.

A close up of the oldest named inn of Burnley, which dates back to Tudor times. The scene is an auction of furniture in 1886. Here, the Churchwardens of the Parish Church conducted the business of the Parish, and partook of refreshments.

The old houses facing the Church of St. Peter were pulled down in 1881 to widen Church Street when the tramway was laid. Later, old Godley Lane disappeared, and the present Ormerod Road began to take shape, as seen in this photograph of 1888.

This shows the junction of Colne Road and Bank Parade in 1900. The Russian Cannons were brought to Burnley and positioned here in 1867 through the influence of General Sir James Yorke Scarlett, K.C.B., whc was known as the 'Hero of Balaclava.' He commanded the Heavy Brigade and while stationed in Burnley married Miss Charlotte Hargreaves, daughter of Colonel Hargreaves, in 1835. The guns were removed and melted down for scrap to aid the war effort in 1941.

This Tudor house was used for many years by Jonathan Whitaker for his trade as a monumental mason, and was known as the Cross House. Chantry priests were believed to have lived there, as there was some evidence of this when the building was demolished.

The 'new' Burnley Centre in 1850 shows the 'Swan Inn' and the 'Black Bull' on the left. The gas lamp in the centre of the picture was known as the "Gawmless"– christened by the locals, no doubt, for its 'dim' or 'ill-lit' performance !

Burnley's early steam trams were introduced in September, 1881, and in their early days the original licence for use did not allow use of steam in Church Street, and several prosecutions for steam emission led to the entire use of horses for some time. Here we see one with trailer tram-car, in the town centre of 1890.

Here, previous to 1866, was held for many years a weekly market. And here too, for many years, did the local polititians meet o'nights to settle great affairs of State. It may be considered as the centre of Burnley, and at one time actually was; and there may yet be seen by the side of the tram-line the old mere-stone which was formerly the centre of the three-quarter mile radius of Old Burnley. Here converge the roads to and from Burnley; for, as in old times all roads led to Rome, so do all our roads lead to the "Gawmless." The Bull Hotel, which stands out so prominently, was formerly the 'Black Bull.' and is so named in the Burnley Improvement Act (1854). This is an entry in the Burnley Churchwardens' Accounts relating to this hotel which shows it to have been long in existence. It reads as follows—"A.D. 1760-1. Paid to Mrs. Nutter, Bull Inn, for proclamation expenses, £1-11s-8d."

Re-named the 'Bull Hotel,' we see here the scene at the bottom of Manchester Road in 1904. The single decker tram was one of the first in service on the Towneley to Manchester Road route. Note how the old 'Gawmless' has been superseded by a tall tram standard carrying the overhead tram wires.

Further views of the centre in 1908. The buildings on the left are still with us in 1972, but are scheduled for early demolition. This picture was taken from the bottom of Manchester Road looking towards Parker Lane and Boot Inn on the right.

Practically the same view as the previous photograph, showing the new line given to the road by widening the thoroughfare on the left.

Looking from the bottom of Yorkshire Street towards Burnley Centre in 1909. The shop of John Taylor, Wine Merchant, was at the top of Hall Street, or Wapping as it was once known. The Hall Inn, on the right, was once used as a theatre and ballroom, and in 1814 'Othello' was performed there. The building shown here is of a much later date.

Opened in December, 1907, the Palace Theatre cost £13,000, and would seat 2,200 people. It was erected by a local building firm, Smith Brothers, and saw revues, varieties, classical concerts, film shows, and Municipal Concerts through nearly 60 years of entertainment.

Behind the Palace Theatre, at the foot of Hall Street, or Hall Rake as it was once known, the district was called Wapping. The name was supposed to be derived from 'Moll of Wapping,' who lived in the area long ago. The house shown here is the 'Old Blue Bell,'. a common lodging house of the 1890's with an unsavoury reputation.

The 'Black Dog. situated at N0. 4 Cannon Street, in the 'Wapping' area, is shown after closure as a beerhouse. Later the building was taken over by Charles Henry Webster, pawnbroker, who was followed by Richard, his son. The white markings on the wall show the height of water caused by floods in the 1860's and 1880's.

Market Hall and Place, 1890. The foundation stone of the Market Hall was laid on the 25th October, 1866, and it was opened on New Year's Day. 1870, by the then Mayor, John Barnes, Esq. The Hall was 180 feet long, 116 feet wide and 40 feet high to the apex of the central roof. The market of Burnley was originally held near St. Peter's Church and is one of the most ancient in the county. A Charter was granted by King Edward I, in 1293-4, to Henry de Lacy, Earl of Lincoln, to hold a market here, and a Market Cross was erected in 1296. In the early part of the present century a Company was formed who acquired a part of the site of the present market and erected upon it shambles and other buildings for market purposes. In 1865 this company obtained an Act empowering them to close markets held in the streets and to build a new market. Within a short time afterwards they disposed of their property and powers to the Corporation, who afterwards erected the above Hall.

Interior of Market Hall about 1896, gaily decorated with flags for some auspicious occasion. Descendents of the firm of John Harrison still sell their wares in the modern Market Hall.

Preparing vegetables and fruit in the Market Place in 1900. This area was principally used by the wholesalers in the trade, and the names of George Crossley, Thomas Moor, Whyatt and Palmer, spring readily to mind. The The buildings shown were on Garden Street, which also housed the well known drapers shops of Warburton, Bond, Stonehouse, milliner Mrs. Roberts, and the public house, Corporation Arms.

The lower part of Howe Street, off Curzon Street, showing the Star Dining Room, c. 1900. This part of the street led to 'Poets Corner,' and the buildings shown are now part of the store of Marks and Spencer.

The 'Thorn Hotel,' St. James's Street, was built on a farm site in Thorn Croft about 1740, and became one of Burnley's best-loved hotels. The photographs were taken c. 1905, and Hepworth's corner was a popular rendezvous in the 90's.

Tailor to the man folk of Burnley for many years, Alfred Cheshire set up business in Standish Street before opening his shop on St. James's Street, c. 1895. The tailor and outfitter who occupied the premises before him, Ralph Holden, was equally well known to earlier generations of Burnleyites. Sailor suits from Alfred's were a must for many small boys in the earlier part of the 20th century !

The Sun Inn, Bridge Street, one-time home of Miles Veevers, the Constable of Burnley, and meeting place of the Churchwardens for relief of the poor. Below is the sign over the door. Mrs. Veever's hams were famous for their quality in 1820, and the Inn had many coach travellers who preferred the homely 'Sun' to the magnificence of the 'Bull.'

Joshua Duckworth's, No. 6 Manchester Road, c. 1896.

The Town Hall and Mechanics' Institution. The foundation stone of the Town Hall was laid on October 24th, 1885. It was opened on October 27th, 1888, by the Mayor (Alderman George Sutcliffe). The total cost of the buildings (including the Public Baths behind) was £55,000. The foundation stone of the Mechanics' Institution was laid by Lord Carlisle on the 25th November, 1851, Colonel Charles Towneley presiding on the occasion. It was opened in the year 1855. The Institution was one of the most successful in the Kingdom, and provided teachers for 70 or 80 subjects, including the sciences, languages, art and technical subjects. There was accommodation for 1,000 students and there were many valuable scholarships attached to the Institution.

Looking up St. James's Street towards Brown Street in 1904, showing Tailor's shop of Strong Bros. The clock is outside the Jeweller's shop of J. H. Dickinson. The flagpole is on the Public House 'The Royal Oak,' kept at this time by Walter Place, a famous local footballer and athlete of his era. The building on the right is Victoria Building, which contained the famous Victoria Opera House and Empire Theatre.

The railway line from Accrington to Burnley Barracks Station was formerly opened for traffic, after approval by the Government Inspector, Captain Wynne, R.E. The first train left Burnley at 7.30 a.m. on Monday, the 18th September, 1848, and in those early days twelve trains each day was a sufficient number for the traffic involved. Bank Top Station, shown here, opened on 1st December, 1849, and this photograph shows the not so busy scene in 1890.

Waiting for the 'Second House' theatres to commence. St. James's Street on a Saturday evening in 1893.

A sad occasion in Burnley's theatre history. The concluding performance at the Victoria Theatre, which closed in March, 1955. Here we see Mr. Jesse Linscott, the Manager, bidding farewell to the patrons. By accident or design, the last play to be performed was 'Hobson's Choice!''

Hammerton Street, c. 1900, showing Cheap John's Bazaar. This was Burnley's first walk-round store. In 1850, Cheap John's was a Temperance Hall. Hammerton Street was named after Philip Gilbert Hammerton, well known art critic, author and painter of the last century, who lived at the Hollins. One of his novels – 'Wenderholme' – written in 1863, dealt with the Holme Chapel district.

The 'Royal Oak' Hotel, St. James's Street, in 1896. On the site of the property shown was the store of Marks and Spencer built in 1935.

There's something about a soldier — Even in 1898! The soldiers are walking on St. James's Street towards Burnley Centre, and are approximately outside Dorothy Perkin's Fashion House.

Keighley Green — on this site a chapel was built in 1787, and Wesley may have preached there when he visited Burnley in 1788, at the age of 83. When the Wesleyans removed to Hargreaves Street in 1840 the old Chapel became a Court House. For many years it was used for entertainments and lectures. In the early part of the nineteenth century the town's Justices met in the Bull Hotel, but the County authorities took over the Chapel and it became the Court House and Police Station. Later on, it became the home of the Burnley Lads Club, and thousands of local lads have spent many happy hours within its walls.

A procession of St. Peter's Church on Gunsmith Lane, leading to Church Street. They are on their way to a Field Day, in 1907. Note the posters in the background.
At one period in history, Burnley was reputed to be one of the most heavily bill-posted towns in Lancashire!

At the junction of Gunsmith Lane and Yorkshire Street we see workmen removing the tram tracks leading under the Culvert. Taken in 1936, this photograph also features the old Keirby Brewery in the distance, part of the Yorkshire Hotel on the left, and Rishton Mill on the right-centre. Originally belonging to O. & J. Folds, Cotton Spinners, the Mill was demolished to make way for the Odeon Cinema, which opened in 1937.

The original Yorkshire Hotel in 1896. General Sir James Yorke Scarlett was quartered here when he was a young Captain of the 6th Dragoon Guards.

The Culvert on Yorkshire Street, showing :—

Top— Single bore, when all traffic, vehicular and pedestrian, used it. Note the narrow footpath. This was taken about 1887.

Below—The same view, but with the addition of the 'Gimlet Holes' which gave pedestrians protection from traffic.

The Leeds and Liverpool Canal, which still flows over the aqueduct, was opened on 1st May, 1796.

The Roman Catholic Church processions were a feature of local religious life in the town for many years, and this photograph shows the Italian Section, prior to their walk in 1906.

The old entrance to Burnley Cricket Field on Brunshaw Road. The ice-cream cart on the left belonged to one of several Italian families, and the names of Mazza, Cece, Pirolli and Tognarelli spring readily to mind.

St. Mary's Roman Catholic Church on Yorkshire Street was opened on 2nd August, 1849, built on a site given by Peregrine Edward Towneley, at a cost of £15,000. A convent was added in 1884, and district schools were opened as follows:- St. Thomas', Meadows, 1877; St. Mary Magdaiene's, 1883; St. John the Baptist, 1894. A Home for Girls opened in Fulledge House from 1890 to 1897.

THE HUSTINGS ON THE CATTLE MARKET, MONDAY, 15th NOV., 1868.

THE HUSTINGS were on the Cattle Market opposite the foot of Elizabeth Street; the building shown on the left is part of Newsome's Circus: the time approximately 11-45 a.m. on a day that was dull even for the time of year. Mr. Richard Shaw, the Liberal Candidate, had been duly proposed and seconded, and had addressed the Meeting. General Scarlett is shown as making his speech.

THE PORTRAITS SHOWN ARE:—

Messrs. (1) Joseph Clegg; (2) Joshua Rawlinson; (3) Thomas Turner Wilkinson, F.R.A.S.; (4) William Robinson (Reedley); (5) Thomas Nowell; (6) Thomas Dean, M.B.; (7) John Massey (who seconded Mr. Shaw's nomination); (8) Richard Shaw of Holme Lodge, the Liberal Candidate; (9) William Miller Coultate, M.D.; (10) Henry

Houlding (afterwards Editor of the *Burnley Gazette*; (11) Francis Hartley (Mr. Shaw's agent); (12) John Sharples Veevers (Reedley); (13) A. Buck Creeke (Town Clerk); (14) Edmund Parker, (Town Crier); (15) William Lomas (Mayor); (16) John Chester Farn

(Editor of the *Burnley Gazette*); (17) James Heaton (Reporter for *Preston Herald* and *Burnley Advertiser*); (18) John Heelis, J.P.; (19) Richard Parker; (20) Henry Milnes; (21) James Roberts, J.P. (who seconded General Scarlett's nomination); (22) John Greenwood of Turf Moor House (who proposed the Conservative candidate); (23) Captain Harry Buck Creeke; (24) Robert Handsley (Conservative sub-agent; (25) James Folds, J.P.; (26) General Sir James Yorke Scarlett, K.C.B.; (27) George Slater; (28) George Slater, Jun.; (29) Rev. Hugh Stamer; (30) Rev. James Butler, LL.D. (Head Master of the Grammar School); (31) Police-Superintendent Samuel Alexander; (32) John Sutcliffe, a Tinner.

THE THANKS of the Compilers of this Drawing are due to many who have helped in its production, particularly to Mr. W. H. D. Flack, J.P., who from his vivid recollection of the scene has kindly checked the structure of the Hustings and the Arrangement of the principal characters on it. It should be noted that, whilst the positions of about 20 people are accurately given, the remainder are placed conjecturally. But no gentleman is represented as being on the Hustings who is not known for certain to have been there. Thanks for the loan of authentic photographs are due to Mrs. Hudson of Highmead, The Trustees of Mechanics' Institution, the Public Reference Library, the Misses Roberts, Mr. George Rohan, Mr. Flack, and others.

SHAW	...	...	...	...	2,620
SCARLETT	...	...	...	...	2,238
				Majority	382
Number of voters		...	...	...	5,545

The Gaiety Theatre was situated on Parker Lane. In 1880, Mr. Culeen erected a large wooden structure on the Cattle Market and presented melodramas, variety, and circus performances. This building was taken down and in its place there opened "The Gaiety Theatre and Opera House". The programme changed for each performance, and provided vivid entertainment for Burnley folk until it was demolished in 1916.

Ha'porth of Black ! Pennorth of Green ! Hot peas always at the ready could be obtained from Collinge's Saloon, situated on the Cattle Market. This shows Mr. Collinge in front of his Saloon about 1905.

A crowd scene on the Cattle Market during the Wakes Week of 1922. Thousands of people visited Burnley Fair durings its stay - it was a must for everyone.

Still on Burnley's Cattle Market in 1930. This shows part of one of the many queues which annually left for the seaside by omnibus. Note the cloth caps, which seemed indispensable at that time - even on holiday.

Towneley Hall. This noble old Hall has a history reaching back to Norman days. The pedigree of the family itself goes even further back - to the year 596 in fact. The foundation of the present Hall probably dates from the thirteenth century, for in 1235 Geoffrey, Dean of Whalley, received the vill of "Tunleia" from his father-in-law, Roger de Lacy. "Towneley Hall", says a well-known Lancashire writer, "is still in the domain which Roger de Lacy gave to Geoffrey the elder in the days of bad King John. Towneley Hall is one of the few instances in the district in which the quadrangular form has been adopted in the building of the large stone houses, and is the largest and most important of those so built." And Mr. Espinasse said of the Hall: "It is just the place which Sir Walter Scott would have delighted to have described, discoursing the while on the fortunes of its successive owners, of whose portraits it contains an unbroken series from the time of Good Queen Bess almost to our own."

The old 'Woodman Inn' on Todmorden Road, taken about 1906.

This photograph adequately reflects the tranquility associated with Towneley Park, particularly in 1909.

Jim Retford, driver of the famous engine 'Mazeppa', which took the train
that ran between Burnley and Todmorden in the 1850's and 60's. At that
time six trains ran daily to Todmorden between 7.30 a.m. and 5.30 p.m.
The same number also left Todmorden for Burnley every day between
7.59 a.m. and 6.30 p.m. Lines from an old poem ran -

  "I've not the slightest dread, indeed
   With thee I've nought to fear.
  Then welcome to they puffing steed,
   Old Jim the engineer."

Manchester Road Station, c. 1908, formerly known as Thorneybank. Opened October 27th, 1849. The
first train ran on November 1st and there was only a single line at that time.

Healey Hall, situated above Springhill Road, on Manchester Road, about 1880. This residence was then the home of Mr. George Eastwood, J.P., and later belonged to Edward James Artindale, of Artindale and Southern, Solicitors. About 1900, Mr. Thomas Thornber, J.P., of the cotton spinning and manufacturing firm of Benjamin Thornber and Sons, moved into the house, and he became an Alderman and a Freeman of the Borough of Burnley in 1909.

Still on Manchester Road, we see the Rose and Crown on the right of our picture and showing the dangerous curves to the tram lines. The old house remained unchanged for many years, but a likely date for this picture would be about 1908.

"Wife for Sale" – It was in this inn, the Tim Bobbin, on Padiham Road, where a Burnley husband sold his spouse for a paltry 2s.6d ! In early 19th century Lancashire, such behaviour was not unique, but we are pleased to report that the man repented and bought her back again the day after. The inn itself was named after the famous Lancashire author John Collier, who named himself Tim Bobbin. John Collier died in 1786, and it was said he wrote his own epitaph twenty minutes before he died –

"Here lies John and with him Mary,
Cheek by jowl and never vary;
No wonder they so well agree,
John wants no punch, and Moll no tea."

GANNOW TOP

'Gannow Top', Padiham Road, showing the junction with Barracks Road. The scene is of a busy morning in 1904, but the shopkeeper, grocer Mr. Thomas Ibbotson, finds time to be photographed.

The gradual transition of the staple industry from cotton to engineering could well have begun with the opening of this building on Colne Road. Known as Platers and Stampers, Limited, this American firm of hardware manufacturers opened their new factory in Cronkshaw Meadow in 1937. It was to provide work for many of Burnley's unemployed textile operatives, and on May 17th, 1938, King George VI and Queen Elizabeth paid a visit to the factory, seen here with the Mayor, Councillor Arthur Green, standing behind them. The well-known figure of Lord Derby, along with the Town Clerk, Archibald Glen, and the Bishop of Burnley, The Rt. Rev. Edgar Priestley Swain, can also be seen.

Birley Place, Hebrew Road, commonly known as Birley Back, c. 1920. Wesleyan Methodism in Burnley Lane had its rise in a cottage in Back Birley Place in July, 1863, when the first Class was formed here.

Now known as Duke Bar, the junction of Colne Road was once known as Hebrew Bar, and an old toll-gate was situated there to collect tolls from Yorkshire bound traffic. The Duke of York Hotel, seen in the centre of the photograph, was built about 1882, and James Ditchfield was the first licensee. The small grocer's shop on the left was kept by Thomas Bate and his family for many years, although the business removed nearer to Barden Lane at a later date.

Sunday, October 22nd, 1905, saw one of the most disastrous fires in the town's history. Lodge Mill, Byerden, or Barden Lane, was a four-storied building built in 1863. Known as 'Birley's', after the Managing Director, Mr. A. Birley, the mill was used extensively for spinning, having 200 operatives and 40,000 spindles. The oil-soaked floors covered with fluff were to prove fatal to the spark that caused damage estimated at £30,000, for nothing was saved, and only the shell remained after two days of continuous burning. It was situated on the site of Haythornthwaites, makers of Grenfell cloth.

The Victoria Hospital.

The foundation of this Institution was laid on May 24th, 1884, the Queen's birthday. It contained 53 beds and 23 cots, and the total cost was £21,578. The Foundation stone was laid by Sir John Hardy Thursby, and it was opened on October 13th, 1886, by His Royal Highness Prince Albert Victor, K.G. The ground - two acres - was given by the Rev. William Thursby. The movement for the erection of the Hospital originated at a meeting held in St. Matthew's Parish, called for the purpose of considering the advisability of establishing a Cottage Hospital. At that meeting Dr. Brown proposed, and Mr. N. P. Gray seconded the following resolution: "That a committee be formed for the purpose of bringing before the town the necessity of establishing a Cottage or other Hospital for the sick poor." The resolution was carried and the following gentlemen were appointed members of the committee: The Rev. R. H. Giles, Dr. Mackenzie, Messrs. W. M. Grant, N. P. Gray, T. Hoghton and J. Langfield Ward, M.A. Shortly after-wards, a representative meeting was held in the Council Chamber, and a provisional executive committee appointed, of which Mr. John Butterworth was appointed chairman, Mr. N. P. Gray treasurer, and Mr. Joshua Rawlinson secretary.

Early records of Heasandford show that Richard, son of Griffin, granted 40 acres of land to Oliver de Stansfield, who had been Constable of Pontefract Castle. To Heasandford, De Lacy added Worsthorne, with all rents and services of its inhabitants. For all his estates in Heasandford and Worsthorne, Oliver de Stansfield paid 2d. a year in rent ! No doubt the lands were originally granted for services rendered. Oliver lived at Heasandford House, and it is believed that part of the original 13th century building still remains. He became a Member of Parliament for Lancaster, and was buried in St. Peter's Church.

Burnley Lane Head, showing the Black Bull Hotel, and the dangerous curve of the tram track, which was to cause disaster some ten years after this photograph was taken.

This photograph was taken within a few minutes of the occurrence, when a young girl and the conductor of the car were killed and seven other people injured. The accident occurred at ten past twelve on December 19th, 1923, and by a remarkable coincidence the car, No. 10, had been wrecked at the very same spot on November 28th, 1919 ! The tram car had been approaching the top of the steep incline from Rake Head, when a descending motor lorry of Messrs. Stanworth Bros., of Barden Lane, skidded on the slippery road, and a collision forced the tram to run backwards, eventually crashing into the newsagent's shop of Mr. Sunderland at 200 Briercliffe Road.

Interior of the weaving shed of the Harle Syke Mill Company in 1905, illustrating a scene typical of the many mills in the district. William West, of this Harle Syke Mill, also manufactured cotton goods at Belle Vue Shed, on Westgate, in Burnley. At the time this photograph was taken there were nearly 90 manufacturers employed in weaving and spinning.

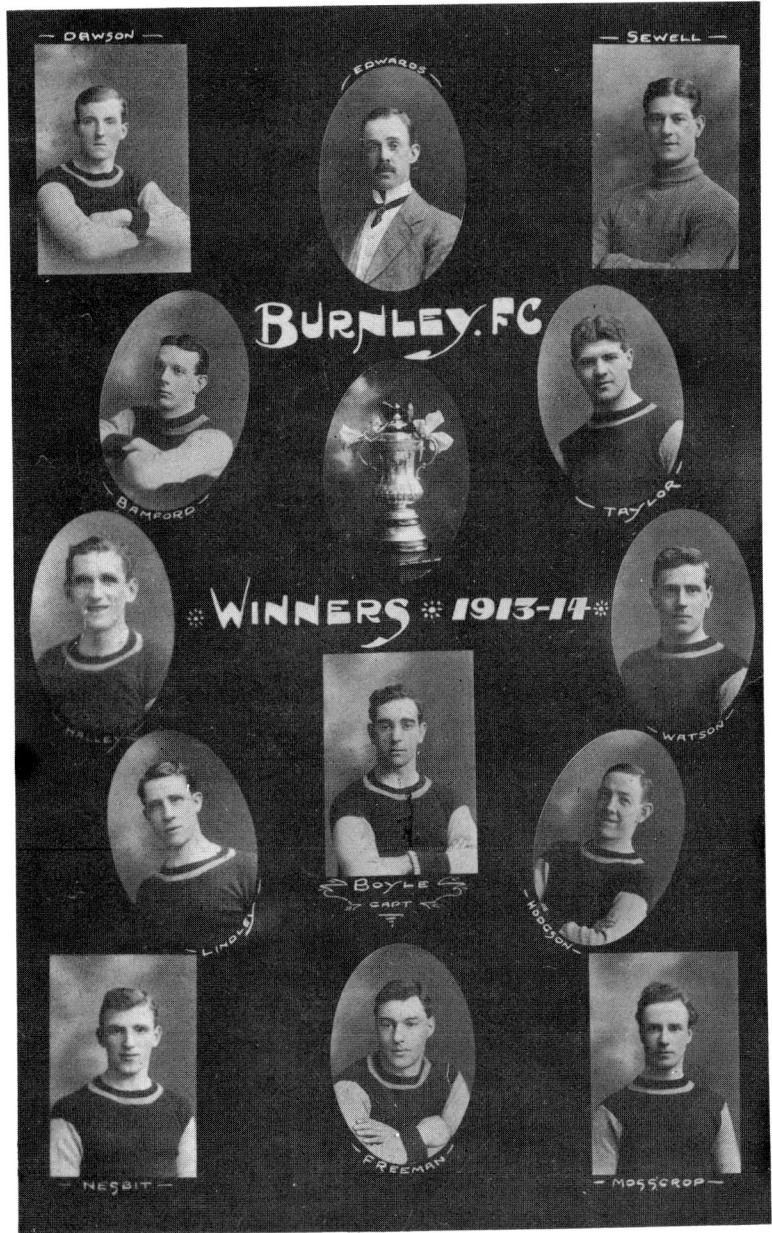

One of Burnley's most famous football teams was that of the 1913-14 season, when the above team won the English Cup at Crystal Palace. Although 'Jerry' Dawson was the regular goal-keeper, he was unable to play in the final tie through injury, and 'Ronnie' Sewell deputised. Dawson was later allowed a winner's medal, and this 1914 Final was the first ever to be attended by the reigning monarch, namely, King George V. Burnley won the match by defeating Liverpool by one goal to nil - the important winner being scored by Burnley's centre-forward, 'Bert' Freeman.

C. W. 182 – built by John Knape, of Bank Top Garage and Motor Works. The 'Habergham' bus had motors by Critchley and Norris of Bamber Bridge, and was fitted with a Crossley engine. It was registered in June, 1906, in the name of F. Groome, motor engineers, of Whalley, who presumably supplied it to the Burnley Motor Pleasure Company. A second vehicle was registered a few days later – C. W. 190. The 'Habergham' could carry 40 passengers, had 4 cylinders and a 40 h.p. motor. It was capable of 15 m.p.h., and fitted with garden seats inside and out. Mr. W. E. Cooke was manager of the Company.

Burnley Corporation's first bus, taken outside Queen's Park main gates. Designed by the Burnley Tramways Department, and built by Leyland Motors, Limited, on a Leyland chassis, they commenced service on Monday, March 17th, 1924. They ran from the Cattle Market to the top of Abel Street, and would seat 20 passengers. The width of these buses was only 6'4", purposely limited to that figure to make them more suitable for the narrow thoroughfares which the vehicles had to traverse. Mr. Henry Mozley was the Tramways Manager at the time the first buses were introduced to Burnley.

"Th'owd Knocker-up with deadly missile", c. 1900, a trade synonymous with the cotton trade in Burnley until the late 1920's.